Be Something
WONDERFUL

WHEN SUDDENLY YOU WANT TO BE MORE

TOM KEARIN

First edition: 2017
Second edition: 2020

Be Something Wonderful by Tom Kearin
ISBN: 979-8676860882

Contents

To all of you who Dare to Be It

Preface

Within you is the entire Universe.
So you really do have it all.

My book begins with a short memoir, laying the groundwork that led to my spiritual awakening and the creation of Be Something Wonderful. Then I talk about the power of the Universe, quantum physics, the law of attraction, and other cosmic principles related to our inherent power within. Finally, I pull it all together with a code to be a better version of yourself.

While I touch on God, the universal laws, quantum physics, and other topics as they relate to our connection to the Universe, I am not an expert or authority in these areas. Rather, the intent is to give you my interpretation of these ideas and demonstrate how they have influenced my life and the creation of Be Something Wonderful.

I have been asked on occasion, where does God fit in with Be Something Wonderful? And the answer is: everywhere. I believe God is that omnipresent, ever-loving consciousness of which we are made and from where we come.

When we talk about the Universe, as big and vast as it is, we are just scratching the surface in terms of understanding the Source of all creation, or God. Before time was, before the

Universe, before heaven and earth—before all of it—there was, is, and will always be the Divine Creator.

In the following pages, I share my own moment of revelation (my aha moment) when that loving energy pushed me to take a radical, new direction with my life. I believe God is within us and that the Creator is always inspiring and nudging us to pursue our dreams and follow our hearts. I believe that that pure, perfect love is not some outside deity; but rather, it's God who dwells within us. I talk about this divinity and its connection to you, me, and the Universe. I also touch on some concepts of quantum physics that point to this divine consciousness that is infinitely bigger, more powerful, and more loving than we could ever imagine.

I believe we were created by God in God's own image and that we are One with the Creator. We are part of that same creative energy that designed and sustains the Universe. Now, that is something wonderful.

Tom Kearin
August 2020

Acknowledgments

Suddenly what you have been just isn't good enough.
You were born to be great, to Be Something Wonderful.

Over the past several decades, we have seen a lot of groundbreaking work around personal growth and spiritual development. Be Something Wonderful and this book wouldn't have been possible if it weren't for those brilliant spiritual teachers and self-help pioneers who have paved the way and whose teachings and methodologies have influenced me greatly and are clearly touched on in this book

Thanks to all of you for your continued insight and inspiration, including, but not limited to, Deepak Chopra, Eckhart Tolle, Esther Hicks/Abraham-Hicks, Gregg Braden, Dr. Lissa Rankin, Louise Hay, Marianne Williamson, Michael Beckwith, Mike Dooley, Oprah Winfrey, Paulo Coelho, Richard Dotts, Rhonda Byrne, Shakti Gawain, Tony Robbins, the late Dr. Wayne Dyer, and so many more. On the shoulders of these inspiring teachers, Be Something Wonderful is trailblazing its own unique path in the life-coaching and spiritual-wellness arena with its compelling brand and contagious message. I am honored and grateful to share the stage with such amazing influences.

I would also like to acknowledge the genius of the early pioneers and scientists of quantum physics, like Albert

Einstein, Max Planck, and Niels Bohr, whom I mention in this book.

And these acknowledgments wouldn't be complete without giving a nod to the ancient spiritual teachers like Buddha, Dalai Lama, Lao Tzu, and others, who knew centuries ago what we are just starting to understand about the Universe, divine energy, and spirituality.

On a more personal note, I would like to thank my older brother Curt and older sister Lori, with whom I am visiting for the holidays as I put the finishing touches on this book. They continue to remind me of where I came from, and in fact, inspired me to reorganize my book at the last moment and expand the memoir section that provides critical insight into how Be Something Wonderful came about.

I would like to acknowledge my father, who passed away when I was just six years old, and my late brothers, Ricky, Danny, Timmy (my twin), and Billy—each having battled through life and each having left this planet much too soon.

In addition, I want to reach out to my mother, who passed away in 2017. It was really only in her final years of life that we saw the mother she always wanted to be. Yet her strength and will to live out her final years with compassion and a renewed sense of motherly love, after a life of struggle and heartache, has encouraged and pushed me to be something more.

Also, I would like to thank my lifelong friend Jack Walsh. Without Jack's friendship and guidance when I was just a teenager still trying to figure things out, I wouldn't be in the amazing place I am today.

Finally, I am grateful to Gesther Aguirre Ortiz (Ges), my confidant and inspiration. Her love and pure goodness are the essence of Be Something Wonderful.

Introduction

*Be Something Wonderful is that burning desire to live your
purpose, to celebrate your authenticity, to start your
journey, to be something more.*

Are you ready for your aha moment that changes your life
forever? Are you ready to discover your divine purpose
and share it with the amazing world that awaits you? Are you
ready to make your inevitable jump into the life you were
meant to live? Are you ready to be something more, to be
something great, to Be Something Wonderful?

No matter your age, occupation, economic status, or
position in life at this very moment, know that it's never too
late, too early, or the wrong time to get started on your new,
transformative journey.

Know that you hold the divine key to the magnificent and
mighty creative forces of the Universe. Know that within your
reach is the extraordinary capacity to embrace your passion,
to pursue your calling, and to live your dreams. Know that you
are an incredible and unique talent, and the world is waiting
for you to share your genuine gifts.

I launched Be Something Wonderful in January 2016 after
a lifetime of having one foot in the spiritual world and the
other in the physical world. This was my aha moment. I knew

then my real journey and spiritual transformation had just begun.

Be Something Wonderful is innovative, authentic, and transformative. It's a goodness. It's a greatness. It's that astonishing creative force of the Universe that you are a part of and share a connection to.

It is the discovery of what you already intuitively know: the unlimited potential in you to be the best version of yourself, to reconnect to the person you already are but have become disconnected from.

The real, authentic you is already perfect, waiting for you to listen, connect, and act.

Be Something Wonderful is my own powerful transformation into the best version of myself. Now I want to share this pure thing with you. Let this be the beginning of your extraordinary journey to reveal your true calling and discover your unique purpose.

The following is a brief summary of what's ahead:

Part one: "Three Thousand Miles Backward" is the memoir of my spiritual transformation leading up to the creation of Be Something Wonderful after more than five decades of kicking around on this planet. It begins in the present day, less than two months after I relocated from South America back to the United States.

This led to my outwardly impulsive decision to hit the road and drive from Southern California to Boston—to visit my terminally ill friend, Jack, spend time with family, and "escape" for the holidays of 2017.

Ironically, this journey of three thousand miles retraced the steps I took twenty-five years ago when I left home in my midtwenties to venture out West. Then, like now, I was in search of something more. Following that, I share some key turning points in my life that have influenced who I am today, and how those led to the creation of Be Something Wonderful.

In part two: "You and the Wondrous Universe," I take you through my own transformation, my aha moment, followed by my spiritual shift and inevitable jump into my new life.

Then we explore your potential to have your own aha moment and reveal your magical connection to the powerful forces of the Universe.

You will also learn about your mind-boggling power to feel good and be joyful no matter your current circumstances.

Later, we touch on the fascinating connection between science and spirituality with a fun and compelling introduction to the world of quantum physics and its relationship with the mysterious creative powers of the Universe. Then we'll delve into your innate superpower called *intuition* and your ability to tap into it at will.

Finally, we wrap up part two with "Unveiling You," a glimpse into your invincible capacity within and the incredible talent and potential you possess.

In part three, we debut the Dare to Be It Code, an empowering key to unlocking your innate greatness. The Code is simply and clearly introduced, incorporating the ten letters of DARE TO BE IT, where each letter represents a fundamental principle. It is your blueprint on how to tap into your God-given superpowers to change your life and to leave your unique mark on this planet.

The Code is your call to action to be the best version of yourself. To be, do, and have anything and everything you ever longed for or dreamed of in your life.

PART ONE

THREE THOUSAND MILES BACKWARD

Crashing in Carlsbad

Be Something Wonderful is about following your inner wanderlust, embarking on the journey of a lifetime.

I laughed. I cried. I peed. And then I drove three thousand miles across the USA. I left Carlsbad, California, motoring across the Mojave Desert, powering through the Rockies, crossing America's heartland, and finally landing in Massachusetts some sixty-two hours later just in time to celebrate Halloween 2017.

I mean, who does stuff like that? Impulsive? Rash? Reckless? Maybe. Let me explain.

Just two months prior to my massive, unplanned cross-country road trip, I moved back to the United States after living and working in Latin America for over twelve years.

While I had traveled between the USA and South America often during this time, reintegrating back into the States full time was a bigger deal than I imagined. I immediately leased a car in Las Vegas, Nevada, where Be Something Wonderful was initially launched and where I called home for a number of years in the 1990s. I then drove to Carlsbad, California, rented a studio, and began my full-time commitment to my new adventure.

It took me some time to adjust and get going with things, including writing this very book that I started months ago and put on hold until now. Less than two months "back home," and while I was still acclimating to the culture shock of being back on American soil, we launched a pilot radio program, producing two promising podcasts. Things were looking up. We finally had signs of some momentum. Then I decided to hit the road. The question remains, why?

The Attunement

Be Something Wonderful is about taking it all in, contemplating the magnitude of the moment.

While in Carlsbad, I begin attending meditation classes and eventually signed up for a Reiki First Degree Practitioner class hoping to boost my spiritual awakening and open up to my intuition and creative juices. It did that and so much more.

After the Reiki training in mid-October, I found myself more sensitive than ever. For a person like me who was already supersensitive, I was feeling and absorbing more of the energy around me, whether it was positive or negative, good or bad.

This makes sense when you understand Reiki. In the certification course, the Reiki master literally opens up your energy channels. This is called *attunement* in the Reiki world. The idea of the attunement is to adjust the etheric body (the electromagnetic energy field that surrounds you and connects you to the energy of the spiritual world) and the physical body to a higher, vibrating frequency.

This opens up the principal energy centers known as chakras, permitting you to channel this life force, or Reiki energy, to help others and yourself.

With Reiki, by putting your hands near or over the body in a certain way, you can channel the powerful life force energy of the Universe to help heal the mind, body, and spirit of yourself or others.

In the days that followed my Reiki course and attunement, I became hypersensitive. More than ever, I felt that my divine purpose and calling was to share the message and mission of Be Something Wonderful.

The "why" of Be Something Wonderful was crystal clear to me: to help others be the best version of themselves. But I continued to struggle with the "how" and the specific steps that needed to be taken to get our ideas into the world. I was encouraged by the pilot podcasts and believed those could be an important part of sharing our message.

But after less than sixty days in Carlsbad, I was still mulling over the direction to take with it.

Sleepless in Carlsbad

Be Something Wonderful is about courageously navigating unchartered waters on a life-changing course filled with mystery, wonder, and delight.

At the same time, thanks to Reiki, I wasn't sleeping well, waking up in the middle of the night with my emotions all over the place. Sometimes I was crying; other times I was laughing. So I decided to take a break and return to my roots for the holidays. My plan was to adjust to my newly awakened self, finish this book, and return to California in January.

While this was happening, I learned that my longtime friend Jack was suffering from cancer, and I wanted to visit him and also spend time with my family. I thought my brother's home on Lake Mascuppic in Tyngsborough, Massachusetts, would be a perfect backdrop to finish this book as well. Looking back, it turns out I was right. So the next morning, I hit the road for Massachusetts to visit my family, see Jack, and put the final touches on *Be Something Wonderful: When Suddenly You Want to Be More*.

Musing in Massachusetts

Be Something Wonderful is where hope overcomes despair,
belief conquers doubt, and love transcends fear.

As I crossed over the state line into Massachusetts, cruising along the Mass Pike (Massachusetts Turnpike for all you out-of-towners), I felt this overwhelming, loving sense of nostalgia. For sure, I had gone home for many visits since the first time I jumped in my car at age twenty-five to go West and get away from it all. Then, I was looking for that wonderful something that would change my life, searching for that missing piece that would magically make me feel better.

However, on this trip, thirty years later, I was not just flying in to do one of my infamous "flyovers" that my friends would often joke about.

Not Just Another Flyover

Be Something Wonderful is about being engrossed in the indescribable glory and splendor of newness and possibility.

What's a flyover you ask? For years, I would fly home for what would seem to be shorter and shorter visits. I was always hopeful that this time it would be different and that somehow I would feel happy visiting family and roaming the stomping grounds of my childhood memories.

Inevitably, I would be disappointed, cut my trip short, and return to the "safe haven" of wherever I was living at the time. However, this trip was different. I was different. Like three decades earlier, I was driving in my car packed with all my stuff. But unlike then, this time I replaced the fleeting hope of contentment with a growing sense of love and compassion for the place, people, and family I abandoned as a young man. This is discussed in more detail in part two. But the simple fact is I have shifted. I am different. I am awakened. I am simply more than I was before.

Figuring Things Out

Be Something Wonderful is knowing that when the fog lifts, you will be further along on your amazing journey toward your dreams.

Ironically, Massachusetts suddenly became the place where I would figure things out and not somewhere to run from. My childhood home would now become my refuge versus a place of painful memories I wanted to escape. It is certain that Massachusetts wasn't any different. My family hadn't miraculously changed. And my childhood memories were still intact.

So, what was the deal? The deal was that I had changed. Suddenly, I wore proudly the scars and wounds of my past. The chaotic childhood no longer had a grip on me. In fact, I was delighted that it now defined me. I knew this was not only about me accepting who I am and what I had been through, but a celebration of it, and the joyous sense that I wouldn't have it any other way. I embraced all of it. The irony is that it took me going three thousand miles backward to remember how far forward I have come.

The real journey is truly an inner one. And until you do it, until you look within for the answers, until you know that you are the only true source of happiness and fulfillment, you will continue to run and stumble along in your life while looking for the answers from outside yourself. You are the only genuine source of love and light in your life.

A Brief History of Tom

Be Something Wonderful is about contemplating the magnitude of how far you've come while imaging the magic yet to be.

It was 1963. JFK was still the president, Martin Luther King Jr. gave his famous "I Have a Dream" speech, Beatlemania was on the rise, and I was born. I came into the world a feeble three pounds and some odd ounces, and I spent my first few months on planet Earth in an incubator, separated from my mother and twin brother. It was an unremarkable start, to say the least.

The Formative Years

Be Something Wonderful is that miraculous twist of fate putting you on course for fabulous and phenomenal change.

At times, having a foggy memory of my past has served me well in terms of running from it and has created many fresh starts for me. But it's a significant disadvantage when trying to write my memoir. My preteen years, as I recall, were anything but happy and well-adjusted. Perhaps that was and still is the new normal: growing up in a highly dysfunctional family. I spent most of my single-digit years sucking my thumb, wetting my bed, hiding under my blankets, and clinging to my twin brother, Tim. I followed him everywhere. Mostly I just existed in his shadow.

I was raised in a family of seven children on welfare and food stamps after my father passed away when I was just six. My mother was left to care for all of us. The glitch was that she was an alcoholic. I am not even sure when that started. Like most things, it probably just occurred over time, a drink here, a drink there, and then more drinks. My older and only surviving brother says my parents were always fighting. This chaos was simply a part of our life growing up.

For me, things were a mixed bag. I have fleeting memories of running behind the big, cushy chair my father would sit on while I was hiding from my mother, who offered up two choices for discipline: the shoe or the belt. The belt was always the softer bet. That said, it still stung. While I am certain my mother's drinking began before my father died, the drinking and chaos definitely became worse in the years that followed.

Of course, she didn't drink all the time. The best times were the first thing in the morning when she was just sipping her coffee. The worst times were any time after that, when she would replace the java with alcohol—while still using the same coffee mug—thinking she was cleverly concealing her addiction. The dysfunction continued while continuing to serve up both good and bad days. I have fond memories of family trips to the beach with my mother and her boyfriend of many years, Ed. Ed was around the family while we were growing up, a sort of father figure to me and the other younger Kearins, but not so much to my older brothers.

As an insecure kid I worried about everything, but mainly about my thin hair. For some reason I feared that I was going bald at the ripe old age of ten. After complaining to Ed about it, he made me feel better by simply saying that I could use his magic hair gel that kept his hair from falling out.

Strangely, I bought the story even though Ed had little hair to show for it. So sprinkled into my tumultuous upbringing were signs of some parenting–even from my mother. She would often share these cliched words of wisdom when I was feeling down: "Where there's a will, there's a way."

Growing up, and as far back as I can remember, I always felt distracted, out of sorts, out in left field, and just plain awkward with my place in the family and in the world. I remember once, while having breakfast during one of our vacation getaways with my mother and Ed, pouring orange juice all over my eggs, thinking I was reaching for the salt. I was clearly in another space and time. A world all to my own.

My teen years were not much different in terms of my odd place in all of this. Instead of thinking that perhaps I was meant to connect with something bigger than my physical self, I wrote it off to just being awkward. Period.

As a teenager, I finally started to step out of my twin's shadow. I was not, however, athletic. When Peterson, the gym teacher, yelled out "ten seconds flat" on the fifty-yard dash, I thought that was good. I mean, "flat" sounded like I crushed it, only to later learn that I was painfully slow. The athletic failures seemed to define my teen years. After I graduated high school, I joined a Kenpo karate studio just a few miles from home. It was a game changer. I immersed myself in the martial arts, earning my black belt in just two years. While I wasn't a natural at any sport, or anything really, Karate taught me that if you practice long enough and hard enough at something, anything is possible.

This was the turning point that pushed me to go to college and eventually graduate with a business degree in accounting.

Before moving on to my later years, I want to share two events that would influence my life and lay the groundwork for my eventual spiritual shift and the creation of Be Something Wonderful five decades later.

As a child and teenager, I was sensitive. I was known as the "sensitive one" among family and friends. This carried on into adulthood, and I became keenly adept at hiding it. It wasn't a great thing back then, but now it's a clear prerequisite for what I am doing with Be Something Wonderful.

In the 1970s, Watergate was all over the news, and my brother Ricky had just returned from reform school as a born-again Christian. Referred to by some as a "Jesus freak," Ricky believed. Soon I did too. Once a week, Ricky would hold Bible studies, where he would point out biblical verses and have us read them aloud. I locked and loaded on this.

Not so much because of the religious aspect or having my own Bible engraved with my name, but because I really wanted to believe there was something much greater and more powerful than my physical life and existence. That there was something divine to turn to for refuge. That was a seriously heavy load to carry for a ten-year-old.

Then one day a small miracle happened.

I lost one of my toys and I prayed to God to help me find it, and low and behold, it miraculously showed up. I was hooked. The sensitive one now believed more than ever.

Then tragedy struck: Ricky was found in his apartment unresponsive and had to be rushed to a nearby hospital. The official report said he had choked on a sandwich. Ricky would eventually lose his fight with life and die at age twenty-three. He was in a coma for weeks, brain dead, as my mother, bothers, sister, and I visited him. As a senior in high school, it was my first brush with death that hit so close to home since my father died, which I was too young to remember.

I prayed. I cried. I struggled to understand why he had to suffer. Why did he have to die? There must be more to life and death than this. What is this all about?

My brother Ricky introduced me to that divine something, that Godly energy, that something more, and while he grasped onto it through his Christian beliefs, I simply knew there was something much more powerful beyond this time and space. I believed. But I wouldn't let it consciously resurface until more than thirty years later.

The Disconnected Years

Be Something Wonderful is the audacity to risk, fail, and then try again—going after it with strength, conviction, and clear vision.

As I approached adulthood, I felt disconnected from family, from friends, and from whom I truly was. I dealt with this as I always had. However, hiding in my room and under the blankets until the yelling and chaos passed was no longer an option. So I simply put my head down and ran for my life—trying to find my way back to that sincere and naive child with innocent curiosity and big dreams. I wanted to remember what it was like before the noise of life set in.

Being raised on welfare and food stamps had its advantages. So by using the full force of student loans and grants available to low-income families, I went to college. I lived at home until we couldn't afford to hold onto the house anymore. I remember studying up in my room with the door shut to keep the ruckus of my mother's drunken rants at bay. Of course, this didn't stop her, as she threw a stapler at my door, yelling at me to quit school, get a job, and be like the rest. But I continued to dig in, stayed focused, and managed to move out and finish university with an accounting degree.

I'm still not sure how exactly why I decided to go into accounting. But I found the structure and the need to balance things comforting. Then, after three years working as an auditor in a Big Eight accounting firm in Boston and as a newly minted CPA, I packed my car and moved to California. Yep, I made a run for it.

Landing in California, I got a job as a financial controller within a few weeks and began my new life three-thousand miles from the chaos and confusion of my childhood home. From there, the company I was with moved to Las Vegas, and this is where I would live for the next ten years or so. I would visit family and friends back East from time to time, being careful not to stay too long. I went back to university to get my MBA and joined a new technology start-up company in the early 1990s.

I then spent the next eight years working with the founder and others to get that promising company off the ground. The story of that failed venture could fill another book, so I will save that for another time while giving you few highlights here.

My business partner, the founder and CEO of the start-up, died suddenly from a massive brain tumor about six years into it. At the same time, we ran out of money. But somehow, we managed to catch the interest of a venture capital firm in Los

Angeles. With the founder out of the picture, they saw an opportunity and swooped in to buy what would later become a controlling interest in the company. As is often the case with things like this, I didn't last long working with the venture firm.

So after eight years of sweat equity, I was out. For the next year and a half, I would work as a consultant and travel a bit while considering my next move. I was lost for a while. For the first time since graduating university in 1986, I wasn't defined by a job title or what I did for a living. This rattled me initially, but eventually, the idea of not needing to identify with a work title grew on me. I looked for other positions during this time, but I wasn't interested in any of the opportunities coming my way. Then Peru came in the picture.

I landed in Cusco, Peru—home of the ancient Inka Empire—in November 2004 while traveling with my good friend Xavier. I loved it. For some reason, I connected with this foreign city. After visiting, I returned to my home base in Las Vegas and decided to move to Cusco the very next month to live, breathe and take it easy for a while. Yup, I made another run for it.

This was another seemingly massive impulsive decision in my life. But somehow it made complete sense to me. While there, I met an American business guy who had started a small language institute in Cusco.

I attended their ESL teacher training course and joined them as an English teacher in February 2005.

This would define my next twelve years as I grew with the organization and became an owner with the founder and his wife.

Interestingly, as I moved up from English teacher to teacher trainer, to general manager, to stockholder, and finally chief operating officer, I resisted each move. Inevitably, though, I would cave in and stay even longer. That "longer" turned out to last more than a decade.

We expanded several times through the years–from the start in Cusco, to Costa Rica, Guatemala, and eventually a small institute in the USA. I became fluent in Spanish and a legal resident of Peru. I enjoyed my time there; however, I always had one foot there and one foot in another world. This would become more visible around the end of 2014 as I grew increasing restless and frustrated.

In the three years that followed I would have tremendous ups and downs. I knew that I was destined for something much greater and more important.

I knew there was something else I should be doing, but I didn't know exactly what that was. It's not at all that I disliked my work, my business partners, or the people I worked with– on the contrary, I loved all of it. I even became one of the three principals in this fun, international, and educational travel company. Still, there was that constant gnawing in my gut that said, "I want to be more."

Yet something huge was missing in my life. I couldn't put my finger on it. I was unable fill the hole I had had ever since my first memories as a child, and the feeling grew stronger each day I stayed in Latin America. I felt suffocated and trapped. My spiritual shift had started.

I became increasingly restless, antsy, and unsatisfied. I confused and aggravated my business partner at times while frustrating myself even more.

As you will learn in part two, the missing piece finally came to light, and Be Something Wonderful was launched in early 2016 while I was still in Latin America with this international organization.

YOU AND THE WONDROUS UNIVERSE

That Aha Moment

*Be Something Wonderful is that momentous moment when
the dots finally connect and your real journey begins.*

There comes a time when you decide to stop letting others define who you are and what you can become. There comes a time when something inside you shifts and you are never the same. There comes a time when you decide to leave behind the old you–the follower, supporter, guardian, and champion of other people's visions and ideas–to pave your own road to greatness. There comes a time when you have such a powerful and profound sense of clarity about who you are and what you can become that you must act on it. That's your aha moment.

Your aha moment is when the dots finally connect. When that restless sensation and burning desire that you've felt your whole life can no longer be ignored. When that soft whisper finally gets loud enough and clear enough for you to hear it, urging you to take the stage, pushing you to step into the spotlight, and inspiring you to put forth your vision. Your aha moment is when the Universe reveals your divine purpose, and you know. This is it. This is my path. This is my passion. This is my journey.

My Aha Moment

Be Something Wonderful is when everything clicks and your bold and brilliant future unfolds before your eyes.

My aha moment surprised me in January 2016 on just another ordinary evening in Cusco, Peru. I was slouched in my chair in the offices of the company where I had been a partner and executive for many years. At the end of a long day, I sat gazing at the screen of my laptop, feeling exhausted and anxious. I mumbled to myself, "There has to be more ... I ... I need to do more ... I ... I need to be more."

As I tended to do from time to time, I doodled my initials on scrap paper over and over again. Nonchalantly carving out the TK and making a swirling circle around the letters all in one fell swoop. However, this time it felt different.

It is clear to me now that on that particular evening, the Universe was eavesdropping on my conversation with myself.

As I stared at the half a dozen or so versions of my initials, I felt this sudden jolt of energy rush through my body. I quickly sat up and began feverishly jotting down my initials again.

This time it was more deliberate, more focused. I sketched my name under the image, all the while thinking about my former business partner from that start-up in Las Vegas, who, when asked what he did for a living, would joyfully respond, "Something wonderful."

This was when it all clicked for me, and Be Something Wonderful was born. The very next day, I began work on the logo design. Later that month I flew to Las Vegas, Nevada, and officially launched the organization. During the same visit, I intuitively filed the trademarks, unclear exactly where it would all lead at the time.

I knew it just felt right, it just felt good. And somehow, I just sensed I was onto something big, indeed "something wonderful."

The Big Shift

Be Something Wonderful is about relishing change while envisioning the extraordinary journey yet to come.

Following or sometimes leading up to your aha moment, you experience an inevitable shift where nothing quite feels the same. It's because you're not the same. You have shifted. You are more than you were. You are growing and evolving at a rate that you have never experienced.

It's the momentum of energy coming from a place where you are aligning with and trusting in the bigger picture. It's about having faith in and hope for what can be achieved when you focus on your dreams. It's a new, growing awareness and clarity of who you are and what you are capable of. It's about trusting in your wisdom and power and sensing that the real knowing comes from within.

It's an activation of your inner godliness, where you begin to trust what deeply and profoundly resonates with you. It's a breakthrough energy that gives you a sense of your higher self and the magnificent connection to all there is. It's a thrilling infusion of goodness and well-being as you embrace what is perfect, beautiful, inspiring, and momentous for you.

It's pure, divine grace rushing through your veins, invading your body, mind, and spirit. It's the beginning of your transformation into the best version of yourself. This is your inevitable shift.

My Big Shift

Be Something Wonderful is about opening your heart to the revitalizing and rejuvenating beauty of all there is.

In late January 2016, I returned to South America from Las Vegas with my newly incorporated company and an overwhelming feeling of excitement, hope, and anticipation of what Be Something Wonderful could be. I felt connected. Inspired. Hopeful. Excited. Loving. I was empowered with the passion and energy of what it represents. The powerful, positive energy of Be Something Wonderful was running through my veins and throughout my body now. I had shifted. Suddenly, I was focused on the bigger picture.

The idea from childhood that I was part of something much more massive and infinitely more important than myself or any one person had returned.

Now as I danced between two worlds more than ever, the challenge was to keep growing and expanding spiritually while continuing to work and live in South America.

For the next eighteen months or so, I eagerly moved Be Something Wonderful forward by laying a firm foundation and business platform underneath it. I brought on an experienced business partner, secured proprietary domains and trademarks, and developed the website and social media platforms—all the while continuing to promote this contagious and powerful message. Of course, the risk was not moving beyond this and getting stuck between worlds, so to speak. I had shifted but would eventually become stalled and stuck.

Unable to move beyond this stage, I was weighed down by the day-to-day responsibilities that didn't include Be Something Wonderful, and increasingly felt the frustration and disconnect of not being totally committed to my new calling and divine purpose.

I had to let go, take a leap of faith, and make the jump into my new life, but when? And how?

The Inevitable Jump

Be Something Wonderful is about making the jump into the extraordinary life you are meant to live.

You have been through your phenomenal aha moment and begun to shift into a more spiritual and fulfilling place. So now what? The challenge now is to keep evolving, expanding, and growing. The risk is falling back into what is comfortable and familiar. Don't let the fear of this insanely delightful, powerful new you cut off your momentum and choke your dreams.

You will return to the same daily routine, feeling unfulfilled, restless, and out of place because you've experienced the thrilling sensation of what it's like when you let your heart strings pull you in the direction of your purpose and calling.

Somehow you just can't take the leap of faith. This is when you need some divine intervention. The good news is the Universe just won't allow you to continue to be stuck between two worlds. You've come too far. That day inevitably comes when the Universe gives you the big push and shove, and you make the jump into your new beginning.

My Leap of Faith

Be Something Wonderful is the comfort and confidence in knowing that something magical and amazing is about to happen.

My inevitable jump came more than a year and a half after I had my aha moment and the launch of Be Something Wonderful. In mid-July 2017, while still running our business in Cusco, Peru, I became increasingly irritated and restless. Yet knowing that I needed to move forward, I still wasn't able to pull the trigger.

Be Something Wonderful was now more than a company with an uplifting message. It represented everything amazing and wonderful to me. It was inside me. I had shifted. I wanted to shout it to the world and give everybody the gift of catching the contagious well-being and inherent goodness of Be Something Wonderful. Yet I was weighed down in South America.

Then it finally happened. The Universe started nudging me. And when it still couldn't get my full attention, it gave me a big push and shove that resulted in my jump and return to the United States to build Be Something Wonderful full-time.

The nudging started with several difficult conversations with my business partner and friend of twelve years, the founder of the institute in Latin America. We had had a few over the years, but this one felt different, bigger. But more likely, it was me that was different.

In any case, I felt it was time to move on. The Universe had different plans for me. I was leaving Latin America, my residency in Peru, and the company I had helped grow. That was it. By Labor Day weekend 2017, I was back in the USA. I jumped with the help of a big, divine push and shove from the Universe, starting my new life and living my dream of Be Something Wonderful.

I Get It Now

Be Something Wonderful is that pure thing—that invincible, benevolent energy field of goodness that connects us all.

I've always loved the 1988 Christmas comedy *Scrooged* a fun, comical, and light-hearted interpretation of Charles Dickens's A *Christmas Carol.* Ironically, as funny as the movie is, I always end up with watery eyes, deeply touched by the ending when Bill Murray's character, Frank Cross, a bitter, cynical television network executive, who on Christmas Eve after being visited by the three ghosts, shouts out, "I get it now!"

The message is a powerful one:

> It's the one night of the year when we all act a little nicer, we, we, we smile a little easier, we, w-w-we, we, we cheer a little more. For a couple of hours out of the whole year, we are the people that we always hoped we would be! It's a miracle . . . I get it now! If you believe in this pure thing . . . the miracle will happen and then you'll want it to happen again tomorrow . . . . . . It can happen every day! You've just got to want that feeling! And if you like it and you want it, you'll get greedy for it. You'll want it every day of your life, and it can happen to you! I believe in it now. I believe

it's gonna happen to me now. I'm ready for it! And it's great. It's a good feeling . . . (Bill Murray as Frank Cross in the 1988 movie *Scrooged*).

No matter how many times I see this movie, the ending never fails to give me goose bumps and fill me with an overwhelming sense of hope and belief in our ability to connect to something so much greater than ourselves. But what is this "miracle" and "pure thing" that Frank Cross is referring to? Next, we explore the intriguing world of quantum physics to help shed some light on this.

Quantum Weirdness

Be Something Wonderful is the knowing that we are all connected to this intelligent consciousness and quantum field of information, energy, and light.

What if it were true? What if you were connected to this vast, invisible, vibrating, conscious energy field? The universal mind. Source energy. Divine intelligence. The quantum field. Or what some call God.

What if quantum physics were right? What if you were powerful beyond measure? What if you could be, do, or have anything?

It is. You are. And you can.

More than a century ago, scientists made a mind-boggling breakthrough proving what spiritual teachers such as Buddha, the Dalai Lama, Lao Tzu, and others, along with the ancient texts, have embraced for thousands of years: the Universe and everything in it is pure, vibrating energy.

That's right, everything. From the physical to the nonphysical, from the seen to the unseen, you, me, the Universe, even a Starbucks coffee, and everything in-between, are all made up of the same stuff–energy or light.

What was previously believed about atoms, matter, and all physical things was turned on its head by quantum physics. Simply put, quantum physics is the study of tiny, invisible particles of matter.

So what happened when quantum scientists drilled down beyond atoms, particles, and matter? They found subatomic particles. And when they looked beyond subatomic particles? They found energy. Pure, vibrating energy. From that, the amazing world of quantum weirdness was born. The lines between science and spirituality were forever blurred.

Planck, Einstein, and Bohr

Be Something Wonderful changes everything, turning your world upside down.

It all started with Max Planck, considered the father of quantum physics, who determined that waves of energy or light are not one continuous wave, but are tiny packets of vibrating energy that he called *quanta*. So now energy waves could be looked at like particles: as discrete lumps of something. Then Albert Einstein followed with his breakthrough finding that all matter is energy.

The chair you are sitting in. The car you drive. The pizza you ate last night. You, me, your cat, the dog. It's all energy. Everything is energy.

Finally, it was Niels Bohr and a group of other quantum pioneers that came along and proved that energy can be both waves and particles, but not both at the same time. Now *that* is weird. This quantum weirdness is called *wave-particle duality*. As a wave, subatomic particles or quanta can take every possible path at the same time.

In other words, this energy can be waves *or* particles until observed. The staggering conclusion is that the stuff you are made of is essentially an infinite wave of possibilities in a quantum field of pure potential. And only when you focus your attention on this wave of energy with your beliefs, thoughts, and expectations do all probabilities collapse, and matter forms. Niels Bohr was exactly right when he said, "If quantum mechanics hasn't profoundly shocked you, you haven't understood it yet."

You literally create your own reality with your consciousness. This isn't fiction. This is science. The Universe and everything in it only exists because you are part of the quantum field of energy, and you literally imagine it into being. With this discovery, Newton's theory describing everything in the Universe as solid matter and moved only by gravity was debunked.

The way the scientific world would look at atoms, the building blocks of all things in the Universe that are both physical and nonphysical, seen and unseen, would never be the same.

What You Now Know

Be Something Wonderful is the riveting realization that we are all made of the same stuff—the miraculous, creative energy of the Universe.

You now know that atoms are made of smaller subatomic particles. These subatomic particles are made of something even smaller, called quanta. And quanta are packets or discrete waves of vibrating energy. So you, me, the Universe, the stars, plants, animals, sound, wind, thoughts, laptops—you get the idea—are all made of the same stuff. We all come from this one source of energy—the quantum field of energy.

You now know that this energy is wave forms of probability in an infinite field of possibilities and that physical matter doesn't exist but shows tendencies to exist until observed. Your thoughts, consciousness, and imagination create and have created all things in your reality, including the Universe you live in.

It Gets Even Weirder

Be Something Wonderful blows your mind.

But how do you know you are connected? If the weirdness of wave-particle duality is not enough to convince you, let's look further into quantum weirdness with what scientists call *entanglement*. Entanglement is what Einstein referred to as "spooky action at a distance." Scientists discovered that when a particle is split into two and then separated by large distances, and it doesn't matter how far, what you do to one particle instantly affects the other particle, as if they are instantly communicating with each other.

But wait, we learned in school that nothing can travel faster than the speed of light. So what's going on? The only conclusion is they don't need to travel to communicate. They are entangled. Atoms, subatomic particles, and the energy that comprises them are all infinitely connected. Which means you, me, the Universe, and, yes, a Starbucks coffee, are all infinitely connected. We are all entangled. Spooky indeed.

This can only mean the quantum field of energy is a connected, eternal, omnipresent consciousness that includes all matter and nonmatter and all physical and nonphysical things that existed, exist, or will ever exist. An infinite source of pure potential of every seen and unseen thing, thought, belief, and intention that ever was, is, or will ever be. A divine consciousness where everything that exists is a product of our thoughts and imagination.

A conscious and intelligent universal mind that each and every one of us is connected to and has at our disposal. Max Planck referred to this as the matrix of all matter: "All matter originates and exists only by virtue of a force . . . We must assume behind this force the existence of a conscious and intelligent Mind. This mind is the matrix of all matter."

You Are a Powerful Creator

Be Something Wonderful is about tapping into the powerful, creative force of your thoughts, feelings, and emotions.

As mentioned earlier, the physical body you occupy that is made of cells is more than just a lump of solid matter. Cells are molecules. Molecules are atoms. Atoms are subatomic particles. And subatomic particles are pure, vibrating energy or light. Furthermore, even more powerful are your thoughts, feelings, and emotions. They, too, are made of the same pure, vibrating energy of the Universe, but carry a much more potent vibration. Like all matter and nonmatter, they carry a unique vibrating frequency that attracts other packets of similar vibrations that join together to create matter, things, or your reality.

You come from the same source of energy that creates worlds. You are a powerful creator. This isn't fantasy. This is science.

Believe It

Be Something Wonderful is about unveiling your extraordinary ability and courage to create a life that is authentic to you.

As Frank Cross in the 1988 movie *Scrooged* happily declared, "I get it now!" Happiness, abundance, and success are not random events, luck, or happenstance. On the contrary, all of it and more is available to you. It's your divine right. Let's be clear: "You are powerful beyond measure." However, it has also been said, "With great power comes great responsibility" (the Peter Parker principle from *Spiderman*).

Are you ready to accept that responsibility? Are you ready to accept and embrace that the events and circumstances of your life aren't the result of random acts of the Universe out of your control? Are you ready to be more? Are you ready to Be Something Wonderful?

Just Because

*Be Something Wonderful is about jumping
for joy just because.*

At the root of everything you chase, everything you wish for, and everything you covet—a big bank account, a loving partner, an adventurous weekend, a happy family, sleeping in, good health, a new car, great friends, fine wine, the dream home, or whatever it may be—all of it, and I mean everything you seek is for the sole purpose of feeling good. So why not just feel good anyway?

That's right. Start there. And then everything else—a meaningful career, being famous, a fun night out, getting rich, the perfect body, traveling the world—is icing on the cake. Because you don't need any of it to feel joy, to be happy, to Be Something Wonderful.

You and only you control all of it. You are unimaginably powerful. You are an awesome creator. Embrace it.

It's Magic

Be Something Wonderful reveals the magical side of life.

Everything in your physical world was created by you. It all starts on the inside. If you feel crappy on the inside, guess what? That's right: you bring crappy into your reality. The source of any problem, no matter how big or how small, is rooted in how you feel. Feel good. Feel joy. And suddenly your problems seem to melt away as if by magic. Well, actually, it *is* magic. And you have access to this magic on a daily basis.

It's who you really are. You are part of, come from, and are connected to this pure, positive, universal energy.

It's that simple. Just drop down into that joyful space where everything and anything is possible. When you do, the people, events, and circumstances that surround you suddenly lose their power over you. What's more, the people, events, and circumstances around you change, magically, to match your happy inner state. Your inner state of joy is no longer dependent on outside influences. You are happy just because. This is when the magic happens.

All of It

Be Something Wonderful feels good.

Call it what you will. Luck. Karma. Law of attraction. Simply put, when you feel good, you are in a state of allowing the Universe to bring you all of it, from your smallest desires to your greatest hopes and dreams. And when you don't feel good, you are resisting the universal flow. You're disconnected from the powerful source energy of the Universe. Everything feels heavier and more difficult. Things just seem to go wrong. So stop chasing joy and just feel good now. Just feel good anyway. Start allowing the infinite source energy of the Universe to flow through you.

Joy, abundance, and love—all of it already exist for you in the here and now. This benevolent source of goodness has always been available to you—waiting for you to notice it, waiting for you to embrace it, and waiting for you to live it.

The Law

Be Something Wonderful is about dwelling in delight, knowing that the Universe has your back.

The law of attraction (LOA) is perhaps the most well-known of the universal laws. Esther Hicks of Abraham-Hicks and Rhonda Byrne, author of *The Secret*, have been two of the most vocal experts on the LOA in recent years. But really, every spiritual teacher from the beginning of time has incorporated an aspect of the LOA in their teachings. So what is it exactly?

The short answer is what you consistently think about and focus on, you attract in your life.

I know what you are thinking: "But I focus on being a millionaire or billionaire, having a dream home, marrying the perfect mate, getting that promotion, starting my own business, etc., but I continually fall short at attracting it into my life. The LOA just doesn't work for me." So what's the glitch, you ask? The glitch is that you need to be happy and satisfied with who you are and what you have in your life in this very instant before you can attract the other stuff.

Lao Tzu taught, "Be content with what you have; rejoice in the way things are. When you realize nothing is lacking, the whole world belongs to you."

Be in love with who you are and what you have in your life right now while holding the other big wishes of your life in view without attachment to actually having them. You trip yourself up when you get attached to the outcome or frustrated with not yet having the other goodies you think you want in your life.

Another consideration is that your thoughts are really rooted in what you truly believe you can have in your life.

Therefore, until your beliefs come into alignment with your thoughts, feelings, and emotions, you won't be able to manifest what you are thinking about continually. This is touched on again in later chapters. Believe it, think it, and feel it, and it will be yours—it's the law.

The Oracle Made Me Do It

Be Something Wonderful is about reflecting deeply,
listening intently, and trusting your own voice.

Listen to yourself! That hunch. That nudge. That tingle. That
itch. That inspiration. That gut feeling. That inner
knowing. That inner voice known as *intuition* is constantly
communicating with you if you would only listen. You just
know you're right but don't know why. It just feels right. That's
your intuition. It's only when you start focusing on how you
feel instead of what to do that you begin to harness your
powerful, eternal, inner self—the divine part of you that is
connected to the source energy of the Universe or the
quantum field.

More Than a Feeling

Be Something Wonderful is the profound feeling that within
you there is something great. Dare to be it.

When we say to focus on how you feel, we don't mean *feel* in
the traditional sense of the word. We are not referring to
feelings such as happy, sad, anxious, angry, or excited.
Because these are just temporary and fleeting states of
emotion that are outer-directed and influenced by the people,

events, and circumstances that surround you and your physical reality. They are not who you really are.

The word *feeling* is commonly used when referring to intuition, for lack of a better way to describe it.

However, intuition is more than a feeling. It's an inner knowing, a state of pure bliss. And this inner state is where intuition lies.

It's a place of joy, peace, and freedom. No external person or influence can affect it. It is a state of simply being. You don't have to do anything to achieve it. It's already there. It's always been there. What's more, you can tap into it anytime and anywhere you want.

Your Intuitive Space

Be Something Wonderful is about leaving your comfort zone and tapping into your innate gifts.

When you are aligned with your higher self, you can't experience anything but abundant love, joy, peace, and a deep sense of lightness. This is your connection to the pure, positive universal energy.

This is your direct line to the quantum field. It is here where you access your profound inner wisdom or intuition.

However, when you let your feelings and emotions take over and allow the outer circumstances to affect you, causing regret, worry, fear, anger, jealousy, or envy, you are out of alignment with the pure, positive source energy that is the divine you. You give up your power to these people, events, and circumstances. Your point of power is right here, right now. And when you let go and stop worrying about the future and regretting the past and give up the need to be right and correct things in the present, you tap into your true, divine, invincible, unlimited self.

This is the only true source of clarity, focus, happiness, strength, prosperity, abundance, and joy. It is from this intuitive space where anything is possible.

It's Not Wishful Thinking

Be Something Wonderful is about harnessing the immense energy, talent, and wisdom that lies within.

Steve Jobs said, "Intuition is a very powerful thing, more powerful than intellect." Why, then, don't you let your intuition guide you in your everyday life? Why do you let your rational, logical, intellectual mind get in the way?

Maybe because this is how you were conditioned as a child. You might remember hearing these common phrases from the adults around you growing up: "Come back down to earth!" "That's wishful thinking," and the classic, "It's a pipe dream."

It's no wonder so many of us have shut off our intuition in favor of the practical, real, and logical. But here's the deal: intuition is the real thing.

It's difficult to know when you are tapping into your intuition or just exercising wishful thinking. However, one way to know when you are connected to source energy and your powerful, intuitive self is to realize how you feel when you are not.

Often when you are not aligned with your higher self and intuition, you feel uncertain, regretful, doubtful, and in general, uneasy about your decisions and actions.

These feelings can give rise to anger, distrust, envy, jealousy, resentment, and even despair. This can only mean you are disconnected from whom you really are, giving your power away to the external influences of the people, events, and circumstances that surround you.

However, when you feel joyful and at peace and are deeply touched by that "feeling," by that "knowing"—that's your intuition guiding you. Trust it.

The Oracle Is You

Be Something Wonderful is the awareness that you are your own teacher. That the real knowing comes from within you.

Anything outside of your inner, divine self can never provide the answer you are looking for. This is true whether it's a solution to a problem or an important decision about what direction to take with your life. External things and people can never make you feel good in any meaningful, long-lasting way. Only when you drop down into that amazing, wonderful space of your inner, divine self, connecting to the pure, positive energy of the quantum field do you get profound, intuitive guidance that comes from a place of pure goodness and joy.

Instead of giving away your power to the temporary and superficial stuff that makes up your physical reality, embrace the profound guidance, wisdom, and pure, positive energy that is the real you. Go to your powerful, divine intuition and watch the magic happen. The truth is the Oracle is you.

Unveiling You

Be Something Wonderful is about sharing your immense talent, unique genius, and inspirational glow with the world.

Right here and right now, you are unveiling the new you. Not because the old you is bad. Not because the old you is not worthy. Not because there's something wrong with the old you.

On the contrary, you are unveiling the new you because you can't help evolving, to become something more, to be something wonderful. Because the new you is the true you. It's the real you.

You are a magnificent child of the Universe empowered with the massive creative energy of the quantum field, blessed with the unimaginable superpower to activate the best version of yourself, and endowed with the divine ability to connect with the higher potential of who you are and what you can become. That's you, unveiled.

Your Divine Gift

Be Something Wonderful is about basking in the radiant beauty, divine light, and absolute clarity of who you are.

You are made up of these small packets of vibrating energy known as quanta. You come from, are connected to, and are part of this infinite, invisible web of energy, light, and information.

This infinitive, intelligent mind contains a record of everything that ever existed, exists, or will ever exist and everything that was, is, or ever will be.

It is here where the magic happens, in this living, intelligent, divine consciousness of probability in the quantum field of possibilities.

Even more mind-blowing is that this sea of energy, divine consciousness, or quantum field of light is a state of pure potential, where particles of matter pop in and out of existence depending on the attention placed on them. The quanta you are made of are in a perpetual state of flux or change, responding to your thoughts, feelings, and emotions, constantly creating and changing your reality.

This is your divine gift: the ability to be, do, or have anything by the sheer will of your thoughts, feelings, and emotions.

Beyond Thoughts

Be Something Wonderful is that firm belief and unflappable conviction that you are part of something much greater than yourself.

Your thoughts, feelings, and emotions are potent quanta, in a constant state of vibration, moving toward and joining with other thoughts, feelings, and emotions that are a vibrational match–creating a new reality over and over again. You are literally in a constant state of creation, affecting your reality with your thoughts, feelings, and emotions.

If all this is true, and it is, why then do so many people continue to struggle with consistently attracting what they desire in their lives? If empowered with this insanely divine and powerful gift of creation, why are you still not creating the life you want? You are meditating. You are repeating affirmation after affirmation. You are going to yoga and spiritual retreats. You are practicing the law of attraction by controlling your thoughts and thinking good things. However, you still don't have what you think you deeply desire and want. So what's the rub?

The rub is that it's beyond thoughts. But wait. What about "Thoughts are things," and, "Whatever you are thinking is what you are attracting"? That's all still true. Thoughts are absolutely beyond a doubt a mighty, vibrating energy force that is a key part of your superpower to create whatever you desire.

However, first you must believe it. Your thoughts are based on what you believe. And just as omnipotent are the resulting emotions and feelings driven by your thoughts and underlying beliefs.

First, you must believe. The belief that you can be, do, or have anything is the paramount starting point. From there, your thoughts based on those beliefs carry the powerful, positive creative juices of the Universe. And finally, as those empowering beliefs and thoughts connect with and give rise to your emotions and feelings, the magic begins to unfold. Feelings and emotions are the language of the heart.

You must "feel the feelings" as if your wishes have already been granted, as if you have already been blessed with your greatest desires.

Believe, think, and feel the feelings and emotions as if your dreams have already come true, and the Universe will go to work aligning the people, events, and circumstances needed to make it happen. Think about that for a minute.

Your important work is to believe. To set the intention. To feel the feelings. To live the emotions as if everything you ever wished for or desired has already been granted. And then to act deliberately with inspired action. Imagine intentionally creating the life you want by simply believing with all your heart that you can be, do, or have anything.

Loving You

Be Something Wonderful is being in love with who you are while embracing the higher potential of what you can become.

The key to having it all is to believe and know you already do. I know what you are going to say, "But I don't have it all. I want more." Okay—fair enough. That's not a bad thing. In fact, it's a good thing to desire more, to want more, and to be more.

However, the "more" that you want will continue to elude you until you lose your attachment to it and believe you have everything you need and want right here and right now. Live as if you have all of your dreams already. Sort of like "fake it until you make it," but just don't fake it.

Be it already. Be that happy, joyful, content person as if all your wants, needs, and dreams have already been granted. This is the key to having it all–believing, knowing, and feeling that you already do. Love yourself unconditionally right now. Then let the Universe do its thing to bring it all to you.

PART THREE

THE DARE
TO BE IT CODE

Introduction to the Code

Be Something Wonderful is about being blessed with the invincible superpower to activate the best version of yourself.

What started as a powerful message has turned into a mission—a call to action that inspires, lifts, and motivates you to be the best version of yourself—igniting that burning desire within to be something more, to be something great, to Be Something Wonderful. The Dare to Be It Code is your powerful key to unlocking your awesome potential, revealing the invincible you. It's the beginning of your amazing journey into greatness—the divine door to the best version of yourself.

The framework of the Code is ten bite-sized principles that start with each letter of each word in DARE TO BE IT.

Following each of these principles are easy-to-follow exercises to help you live and practice the Dare to Be It Code. Dare to be it!

Dare to Face the Fear

Be Something Wonderful is about traveling by your own inner light, welcoming the fear of the unknown with open arms.

In the moment that you face your greatest fears, in the instant that you stand up to those things that you're most afraid of, the feelings and emotions resulting from those fears lose control over you. You are no longer paralyzed by the anxiety of the unknown.

No more are you overcome by the doubt, despair, or threat that something will go wrong or that you will fail in your life or at the things that matter most to you. The most powerful way to stand up to fear is to feel its opposite, love.

When you stand in the pure essence of love, experiencing the loving feelings of joy, happiness, and compassion, fear loses its grip on you.

Gregg Braden, *New York Times* best-selling author of *The Divine Matrix* and *The God Code*, among others, teaches that the ancient traditions only recognized two principal emotions—love and the absence of love—in this case, fear.

Braden declares, "When we have our thought, we are either breathing love of that thought or fear of that thought to create the feeling. And then the feeling becomes sadness or joy or compassion or anger."

When you try to run from fear, eliminate fear, or ignore fear, you create more fear—the fear of being afraid—making fear bigger and the hold on you more powerful and intense. You continue to feed it, so it always comes back for more.

You forget that being afraid serves an important role in your life and in your being. Fear is a reminder that you are not loving yourself enough.

Fear is the wake-up call that you are falling out of alignment with your higher self. Fear is the alarm bell urging you to return to that space of love, hope, joy, and inspiration. Fear is a critical part of your growth toward love.

One of my most challenging bouts with fear was just before making the jump to Be Something Wonderful when I was in South America. I was hopeful in one moment and doubtful the next, joyful then disappointed, and happy then sad, etc. It was an emotional roller coaster.

At first, I was fighting it—trying to force myself to not "feel" these fear-based feelings. I was trying to convince myself that now that I was in the midst of my spiritual transformation, and had shifted, I shouldn't, couldn't, and wouldn't feel fear. That those days were long gone. Of course, I was wrong.

I was empowering fear and forgetting about the much more potent effect of love-based emotions. We need to go through darkness. We need to feel fear. It is the indicator that something is off and we need to make an adjustment.

That's when the switch finally flipped on for me. I got it. I understood. I became familiar with fear—knowing that it was a powerful and necessary reminder that love was, is, and will always be the most powerful answer to overcoming fear and diminishing its hold on me.

I got comfortable with doubt, anxiety, disappointment, and all the rest. Now when these emotions set in and darkness comes, my first impulse is not to run and hide, but to let them coexist for a moment with love, the moment inevitably passes quickly and the exponentially more powerful emotion of love replaces fear.

Allow the thoughts and emotions of fear to be present, feel the associated feelings of doubt, worry, and anxiety, and then let it all go in that moment. Welcome it all with open arms, making the conscious and intentional decision to feel the fear, to embrace the resulting feelings and emotions, and then to replace it all with the invincible emotion of love.

Love leaves no opening for fear and is infinitely more powerful than fear. Dare to feel massively the amazing freedom and power of surrendering to love.

Exercise 1 - Fear

Be Something Wonderful is that thrilling sensation of facing the fear and taking the plunge.

For your first exercise, instead of fleeing from fear, you are going to invite it in, and Dare to face the fear.

1. Close your eyes. Take three deep breaths as you focus only on your breathing for a few moments, deeply inhaling through your nose and exhaling through your mouth.

2. After your third breath, invite fear in. Pick something personal to you that causes a fear-based emotion. It could be doubt or anxiety about money. Maybe it's jealousy or envy of someone. Or it could be something you are afraid of confronting. Welcome it in.

3. Deliberately and consciously feel the feelings of this fear. Say to yourself or out loud three times, "I dare to face the fear."

4. Now, replace this fear with love. Keeping your eyes closed, take three deep breaths again through your nose and out your mouth. On the first breath, while inhaling, think of the fear you invited in, and on the exhale, release that fear, blowing it away as you exhale. Say to yourself or out loud, "I release this doubt. This doubt no longer has a grip on me."

On your next two breaths, while you inhale, think of a loving thought. If your fear was lack of money, think of abundance and prosperity. If your fear was anger over a situation, think of a joyful moment or experience. As you exhale, think about spreading and sharing that love with all those in need. Say to yourself or out loud, "I share this love with all those in need."

Align with the Pure Goodness of the Universe

*Be Something Wonderful by aligning with the power,
strength, and grace of the Universe.*

Once you align with and connect to the highest vibrations of the Universe—overwhelmed with the abundant emotions and feelings of love, kindness, and compassion—you can't help but attract the people, events, and circumstances that match your higher vibration. The transformation can be uncomfortable and even painful as your heart expands and you shed the all-too-familiar lower-vibrating emotions and feelings of worry, lack, envy, and anger.

This divine state of well-being flooded with joy, love, and peace just feels good. It just feels right. And this is when and where the magic happens.

Esther Hicks, speaker and author and probably best known as the channel for the nonphysical entities called Abraham, urges you to choose "unconditional alignment." The idea is that you should make a conscious choice to shift your thoughts and feelings to "feeling better" without waiting for the corresponding outer conditions to change.

What Hicks is referring to here is unconditional love. Choose to love first. Feel good anyway. Then your outer circumstances and the people you attract can't help but to match your new, powerful, loving vibration. In other words, feel good and joyful now despite your physical reality. Then your physical reality has to shift to match your new, unconditional alignment with the pure, positive energy of the Universe.

Aligning was difficult for me at first. I found that I would often default to the seemingly easy choice of frustration, anger, envy, jealousy, disappointment, wanting to be right, and other feelings of being out of alignment. I grew up in an environment where being dysfunctional and out of alignment with the goodness of the Universe was the norm. Dysfunction felt familiar to me. So I knew it would take me great effort to turn this around. Interestingly, it was difficult until it became easy.

Once I changed the default to feeling good versus anything that was the opposite, things took off. Ironically, feeling good, which is really a form of love, has much more momentum than feeling anything but good or joyful. So once I got a handle on that, it snowballed to the point where feeling out of alignment was no longer my default feeling, and it no longer felt comfortable to me.

With an absence of love and the feelings it creates, you leave an opening for the emotion of fear and its lower-vibrational feelings of frustration, regret, jealousy, and resentment. However, when you are drenched in love, there is no room for anything else. Vibrate higher.

Dare to align with the feelings of bliss, delight, and blessedness that result from the powerful emotion of love, and watch as your life changes.

Exercise 2 - Alignment

Be Something Wonderful replenishes, renews, and restores—reconnecting you to that fearless and loving center.

For exercise 2, you are going to make "feeling good" your default state of being.

1. Close your eyes. Take three deep breaths as you focus only on your breathing for a few moments, deeply inhaling through your nose and exhaling through your mouth.

2. Keeping your eyes closed, picture a brilliant, white light coming down from above and surrounding your entire body. Feel the warmth, beauty, and divine goodness of this light.

3. Now, repeat to yourself or out loud, "I feel amazing. I am invincible. I am perfect." You can also replace these phrases with any three highly positive phrases you like.

4. This time take three deep breaths again, inhaling through your nose and exhaling through your mouth. As you are exhaling, repeat, "I am feeling amazing. I am invincible. I am perfect."

5. Do this at least once a day, when you wake up, before you go to bed, or anytime you find yourself falling out of alignment. Notice how you feel when you do these exercises. Let this state of feeling good become your default state of being. Then whenever you fall out of alignment or you feel off, you can immediately return to your delightful default mode of feeling good again.

Release the Old, Making Room for the New You

Be Something Wonderful is about letting go, making room for the Universe to orchestrate new and amazing things for you.

You are meant to grow, evolve, and blossom into the powerful leader you are destined to be, taking charge of your own life, being the CEO of your own path, forging your own destiny, doing what you dream of doing, and being who you long to be. The magnificence of who and what you are is already inside you and has always been there. This pure thing of which you are made is waiting for you to unlock it, expecting you to unveil it, urging you to tap into it—allowing the invincible, incredible, and brilliant you to shine.

Unless you cast aside the past and the associated old, fear-based thinking, you remain a prisoner to your fears, seemingly hamstrung and helpless to move forward, to grow, to expand, and to love. So take the critical step of starting with loving thoughts. Drench those loving thoughts with the powerful emotion of love, and then feel the feelings of kindness, compassion, joy, and peace.

When you are empowered with love and embody the associated loving feelings, there is no more room for your past, fear-based thinking to enter, and the real, loving you emerges.

Deepak Chopra, world-renown author, teacher, and spiritual guru, believes that you must let go of your fixed and limited view of reality to allow a new reality to take its place. And that when you try to hold on to anything, "it is like holding on to your breath. You will suffocate."

It's only when you let it all go that you open the door for the Universe to bring it all to you, everything you desire and want. Fear is about hanging on. Love is about letting go.

My most prominent example of letting go of the past was when I finally made the jump back to the United States after twelve years of living and working in Latin America. Although I was already into Be Something Wonderful for a year and a half, I still couldn't fully let go of my work and life down there. Finally, with help from the Universe, I made a complete break to focus exclusively on Be Something Wonderful, making room for the Universe to bring me new and exciting things.

Once you release the old and get a taste of the boundless freedom of this pure thing, the old emotions and feelings of fear and doubt won't feel right to you anymore. You will reject them. There will be no room in your new world for them.

What's more, the people, events, and circumstances that no longer share in your new, pure state of being fall to the wayside and are no longer part of your journey. Dare to cast aside the past, paving the way for your new, amazing life.

Exercise 3 - Release the Old

Be Something Wonderful is about transcending the old—evolving into the beauty, brilliance, and splendor of who you are meant to be.

For exercise 3, you will practice clearing the old, opening up the floodgates for the new to pour into your life.

1. Close your eyes. Take three deep breaths as you focus only on your breathing for a few moments, deeply inhaling through your nose and exhaling through your mouth.

2. Get three blank sheets of paper and write one thing from the past that you would like to release and let go of on each piece of paper. It could be a grudge, a bitter experience, a sad memory, or a hurt feeling.

3. Starting with one piece of paper at a time, read to yourself or out loud, "I release_____." Fill in the blanks with the thing you want to let go.

4. Now rip each piece of paper into the smallest pieces you can and throw them away in the trash.

5. Close your eyes again, take three deep breaths, inhaling through the nose and exhaling through the mouth, and say to yourself or out loud on each exhale, "I now make room for the Universe to bring new and wonderful things into my life."

Embrace the Everyday Magic of Life

*Be Something Wonderful is about immersing yourself in
the everyday magic and majesty of life.*

Wake up every morning expecting miracles, anticipating synchronicities, embracing the everyday magic of life. Once you realize and accept that you are literally part of the Universe's playground of miracles, you will want to frolic and play in it every day. Instead of being a bystander to the miracles and synchronicities of life, immerse yourself in the pure, positive energy of the Universe.

Look for the signs and go with the flow. Have fun creating your own magic. You are, after all, the magician of your own life. The designer of your own path. The creator of your own destiny.

Richard Dotts, author and spiritual teacher, in his book, *The Magic Feeling Which Creates Instant Manifestations* describes the Magic Feeling as "a euphoric feeling of peace and well-being that lets you know you are on track and connected with the greater part of you."

When you are connected to the source energy of the Universe, you feel this overwhelming sense of joy, peace, love, and gratitude, and it is from this pure state that you can manifest anything you truly desire in your life. In other words, it's your magical inner state—your direct connection to the real you and the powerful, creative forces of the Universe. This is where miracles are manifested and when the magic happens.

For me, things really started changing after I had my aha moment and started Be Something Wonderful.

While I know my shift and spiritual transformation had begun long before then and maybe had been dormant most of my life up to that point, I definitely was more awakened and tuned into the universal goodness once Be Something Wonderful was in the picture.

I simply began to feel this sense of peace, calm, and love that I never really felt on a consistent basis prior. I was finally connecting to that magic feeling. Things started unfolding in the most marvelous way, having the miraculous wind of the Universe at my back.

So rather than continue to walk through life as a victim, thinking that you are powerless to change your fate and current reality, wake up to the fact that in this very moment, you are creating the next moment, and the next, and the one after that, and so forth and so on.

Replace the expression "as fate would have it" with "as I wish it." Stop "overthinking" and start "overfeeling" by dwelling in the inner state of peace, love, and joy. Embrace the magic of the Universe, your higher self, and the real you.

Exercise 4 - Embrace the Magic

Be Something Wonderful is being present, mindful, and conscious of your magical world in which subtle miracles abound.

In exercise 4, you are going to have fun frolicking in the extraordinary, magical playground of miracles called everyday life.

1. Close your eyes and take three deep breaths as you only focus on your breathing for a few moments, deeply inhaling through your nose and exhaling through your mouth.

2. Keeping your eyes closed, picture a brilliant, white light coming down from above and surrounding your entire body. Feel the warmth, beauty, and divine goodness of this light.

3. Now repeat to yourself or out loud, "Just for today (or tonight or this afternoon), I am going to look for the synchronistic signs of the Universe." Whether it's a message from Spirit with a number sequence like 111, chance meetings, or pennies or other coins suddenly appearing, look for the signs and dwell in possibility.

4. As you go out into your day, play in the magic of the Universe. If you find yourself in a long line at a store or bank, imagine another line opening up and you getting called over. If you are looking for a parking space, ask the Universe. Simply put out that peaceful and loving intention, and watch how the people, events, and circumstances change around you to deliver what you need. Remember that there are no coincidences—you are connected!

Trust and Love Yourself No Matter What

Be Something Wonderful inspires you to take risks, feeling the freedom of your boundless potential.

Trust in your powerful connection to the divine and benevolent energy of the quantum field. Set the intention. Ask for what you want. Take the spiritual leap of faith from the invincible position of love and watch as the Universe goes to work putting the people, events, and circumstances in your path to make it all happen.

Know that the Universe always has your back and that when you are in an unconditional state of trust and love, and not dependent or attached to the outcome of your wishes, this is when the magic happens and it all comes to you, from your smallest wishes to your greatest hopes and dreams.

Underlying most spiritual teachings is the idea of trusting and loving yourself unconditionally. The ancients said this about love and trust: "It always protects, always trusts, always hopes, always perseveres" (1 Cor. 13:7 NIV).

As I mentioned at the beginning of my book in the preface, I believe God is within us and that we are all connected. God is love. We are love. Trust love unconditionally.

Trusting myself fully and unconditionally is a wonderful work in progress. Having said that, once I launched Be Something Wonderful and took the leap in committing to it full time without the safety net of my work in South America, I finally dared to trust myself unconditionally.

Trust in the Universe. Love and trust yourself unconditionally. Feel the powerful and invincible feelings that anything is possible. Trust your power and perfection within.

Stop second-guessing and start trusting yourself unconditionally. Know that if it hasn't already happened, your greater purpose and why you are here will be revealed to you in its own time. Remember that you are already perfect. It's not about what you have done, but what you can do. It's not about changing who you are, but rather discovering who you can be. Dare to look inside and see the powerful, loving you that is anxious to show the world what he or she is made of.

Exercise 5 - Trust

Be Something Wonderful is about rising above doubt, worry, and fear, showcasing your eternal luster and glorious glow.

For exercise 5, you are going to immerse yourself in total, unconditional trust in yourself and the Universe.

1. Close your eyes and take three deep breaths as you only focus on your breathing for a few moments, deeply inhaling through your nose and exhaling through your mouth.

2. Applying what you learned from exercises 2 and 3, you are going to align with the benevolent source energy of

the Universe, dropping down into that place of peace, love, and joy.

3. Keeping your eyes closed, picture a brilliant, white light coming down from above and surrounding your entire body. Feel the warmth, beauty, and divine goodness of this light.

4. Now you need to tackle doubt. Once you deal with doubt, you open up the way for unconditional trust. Doubt is a fear-based emotion. So like you learned to deal with fear, you will deal with doubt. Get three blank sheets of paper and write one thing you doubt about yourself–this could be in any area of your life.

5. For example, "I doubt that I will get that amazing job promotion."

6. With each item of doubt, put a big X through what you have written. Below it, write exactly the opposite using *trust* instead of *doubt*: "I unconditionally trust in myself and the Universe that I will get that amazing job promotion."

Now, read each one three times. Absorb the message. Replace *doubt* with *trust* whenever that fear-based emotion enters your space.

Open Up to Your Innate Gifts

Be Something Wonderful is that invincible glow of greatness as you bring in the wholeness of who you truly are.

When you are in your purpose, anything is possible. Your latent talents are begging to be discovered, tapped, and explored. Dare to be outrageously happy and passionate about what you do every day. Be bold. Be brash. Be boundless. Find that spark that turns into a raging fire of courage, curiosity, and creativity. Your magnificent, intrinsic genius awaits you now in this very moment.

Imagine jumping out of bed every day to do what makes your blood pump faster, your heart beat stronger, and your soul soar higher.

Take the plunge right now into your purpose, passion, and destiny.

Tony Robbins, author, entrepreneur, business and life coach, and self-help guru, turned his innate gifts of communications, sales, and people skills into a lifetime of helping others. He declared, "The real joy in life comes from finding your true purpose and aligning it with what you do every single day."

Tony Robbins has shown that with unbridled confidence, unlimited desire, and laser-like focus on your God-given gifts, anything is possible. Robbins is a true rag-to-riches story and self-help hero.

Before I immersed myself in my true passion of Be Something Wonderful, I spent more than three decades in business. I started as an accountant and financial guy and then moved to business operations.

Later, I went to South America to teach and train others to teach, and eventually found myself back in business operations. Throughout this entire time, I continued to have that empty part of me, that hole that got bigger and bigger as the years went by, until the Universe intervened and pushed me in the direction of my passion and purpose, and into what I love doing each and every day.

Remember that you have the immense, invincible wind of the Universe at your back. You are blessed with genuine skills, abilities, and talents yet to be discovered and embraced. There never was, is, or will be another person with your unique blueprint. Dare to do what you are destined to do and to be who you are destined to be.

Exercise 6 – Your Innate Gifts

Be Something Wonderful is about creating your own masterpiece—finding your unique place among the painters, poets, and prophets.

In exercise 6, you will practice discovering what your unique talents and strengths are.

1. Close your eyes and take three deep breaths as you focus only on your breathing for a few moments, deeply inhaling through your nose and exhaling through your mouth.

2. Now get a piece of paper, divide it into two columns, and write at the top of column one: three things I am passionate about and love to do.

3. In column one, write down the three things that immediately come to your head and are very obvious to you. They might even be things that friends, family, and even strangers have alluded to with comments such as, "You are such a good writer. Have you ever thought about writing a book?" for example.

4. In column two, write down next to each passion why you love it. For example, "It is creative," or, "It gives me joy."

5. Look at your sheet of paper and think about whether you are incorporating your passions into your life on a regular basis. If the answer is no, make a plan to incorporate what you are passionate about into your everyday life. It could even mean making your passions part of your career or work as well, if they aren't already.

Believe You Can Have It All

*Be Something Wonderful is about having faith and hope.
It's trusting in the bigger picture. It's seeing the higher
potential of what you can achieve.*

Believe and know that anything is possible when you lead your life boldly with focus, clarity, and purpose. And as Abraham-Hicks and many other spiritual teachers have declared, "You can be, do, or have anything you want or desire." It all starts with your beliefs.

Beliefs are perhaps the most potent ingredient when manifesting anything you want in your life.

Beliefs are how you see the world—your perception of life and reality, and what you consider to be true or real based on everything you have been through or experienced. Beliefs are the creative seeds of the Universe. Therefore, you must ask yourself, what seeds have you planted? If they are anything but beliefs of how amazing and gifted you are, and that you truly can be, do, or have anything, then it's time to stop watering and cultivating those negative, limiting beliefs.

Oprah Winfrey, producer, talk show host, actress, philanthropist, and much more, is a true American success story and a quintessential example of the massive power of beliefs. Winfrey advocates, "You become what you believe, not what you think or what you want."

She reinforces the idea that beliefs, negative or positive, good or bad, conscious or subconscious, are responsible for where you are in your life and what you believe to be true for yourself.

When I arrived at my older brother's house at the end of October, I showed him Be Something Wonderful and walked him through what I was creating. His response really tells the story of how limited beliefs can develop from your childhood environment and stay with you your entire life unless you make a drastic and intentional 180-degree turn to change it all. I told him that Be Something Wonderful was about being the best version of yourself, following our dreams, and leading the life you always wanted to live. His response was a classic Kearin view: "What! A better version of yourself. I'm just trying to survive." And there you have it.

The ultimate limiting belief coming from my own flesh and blood. Of course, my brother is doing much better than just surviving. He has a solid small business and a nice house on the lake.

Yet he believes he is just getting by, and to move beyond any of that is unimaginable to him. I grew up in the same household as my brother and indeed shared very similar "survival mode" limiting beliefs for years. It took me getting in my car at age twenty-five and driving across the country to California to begin my transformation to something much more—ironically, it still took me decades to find my way, and of course it's a continual work in progress.

Now it's time to examine *your* beliefs, digging up the ones that are negative and letting them die with the past. Grow a new, empowering garden of invincibility, clarity, success, abundance, love, and joy.

Clear away negative beliefs based on where you have gone, what you have done, and who you have been. Instead, create and shape your beliefs based on who you want to be and what impact you want to have on the world. You truly are an amazing powerhouse of goodness and possibility.

Begin today to purposely and willfully change and shape your beliefs from hopeless to hopeful, from inadequate to omnipotent, from the impossible to the possible. Dare to start planting and watering the seeds of greatness, those empowering and invincible beliefs that will make your dreams come true.

Exercise 7 - Believe

Be Something Wonderful is the wisdom and clarity of knowing your beliefs and thoughts create worlds.

For exercise 7, you are going to brainstorm and then look at your most prominent beliefs about yourself.

1. Close your eyes and take three deep breaths as you focus only on your breathing for a few moments, deeply inhaling through your nose and exhaling through your mouth.

2. Now get a piece of paper and jot down six firm beliefs you have about yourself. Think in terms of areas of your life to help you brainstorm, for example, family, friends, work, career, and relationships.

3. Look at your beliefs. Next to each belief, label it positive or negative. How many of the six beliefs are negative? If it is more than one, then you have clear limiting beliefs that are slowing your growth and advancement into the amazing life you deserve.

4. With any negative belief, cross it out and rewrite it. You will be so amazed at the baggage you may be carrying.

Repeat this exercise with other beliefs. You will be amazed at the baggage you may be carrying.

Energy Is Everything, Everything Is Energy

Be Something Wonderful is about expressing your immortality, reflecting your inner grandeur and glory for all the world to see.

Scientists now agree with what spiritual teachers, healers, and gurus have believed for centuries–that you, me, and everything around us are all made of the same stuff–the pure, positive energy of the Universe. We are all infinitely and divinely connected. And when you are aligned with and harness this powerful source of goodness and well-being, life unfolds before your eyes in the most beautiful and spectacular way. Your wishes are granted. Your dreams come true. Everything falls into place as if by magic. Indeed, you have the magic of the Universe seemingly at your beck and call.

The late Dr. Wayne Dyer, internationally renowned motivational speaker, author, and spiritual pioneer in the personal growth field, spoke of the Universe being perfect in every way, and when you let go and flow with the universal energy, you become part of its "perfect rhythm."

With this divine connection, you no longer see coincidences as random events, errors, or mistakes, but as synchronicities and divine events of the perfectly operating

Universe that you can manifest at will. Dyer put forth, "Remind yourself that aligning with spiritual energy is how you will find and convey the genius within you."

On the other hand, when you engage fear instead of love, lack instead of gratitude, and animosity instead of compassion, you veer off course and lose your divine alignment to your higher, benevolent, and infinitely powerful self.

Your emotions and feelings act as an alarm bell sounding, as you immediately begin to feel sadness, anger, despair, and even hatred.

These are the warning signs that you need to shift your alignment immediately and reconnect to the goodness and well-being from which you come, and of which you are made—the pure, positive energy of the Universe.

As soon as I feel I am veering off course, I know it. I feel it in the pit of my stomach. What I thought was normal—a heavy, negative feeling in my center most of the time—is anything but normal. Now, the light, benevolent, joyful feeling at my center is the new "normal." So when a negative feeling or emotion sneaks its way in, it now hits me like a ton of bricks, and I quickly return to my benevolent center.

Accept right now in this very moment that you come from and are made of the awesome creative energy of this perfect and beautiful Universe. And instead of believing things just happen to you by chance, embrace the fact that you have been blessed with the divine ability to create the life you want and to influence, shift, and change events in your everyday life at will.

Dare to harness your extraordinary capacity and potential within to shape your world.

Exercise 8 - Energy

Be Something Wonderful is that breakthrough energy running throughout your body, signaling the great things to come.

For exercise 8, you are going to practice harnessing your inherent connection to the powerful source energy of the Universe, similar to what you learned in exercises 2 and 4, but this time making three wishes.

1. Close your eyes and take three deep breaths as you focus only on your breathing for a few moments, deeply inhaling through your nose and exhaling through your mouth.

2. Keeping your eyes closed, picture a brilliant, white light coming down from above and surrounding your entire body. Feel the warmth, beauty, and divine goodness of this light.

3. Now, get a piece of paper and write at the top, "My Three Biggest Wishes for My Life." Jot down your three greatest wishes.

4. Close your eyes again and visualize the infinite, universal source energy and light running throughout your body, filling you with love and joy. Returning to your wishes, focus on how you would feel if these wishes came true—feel the associated feelings of your wishes coming true.

5. Finally, with these feelings engaged, visualize yourself in the specific wishes as if they have already come true.

Intuition Is Your Superpower

*Be Something Wonderful is about embodying the
magnificent and magical power of your intuition.*

It's a subtle feeling, a gentle nudge, a quiet voice, a soft push, and even a warm sensation telling you that you are on the right track, you are headed in the right direction, you are forging your true path. This is when you are tapping into your fearless, intuitive compass. It's your higher self giving you guidance, showing you the way, leading you to your genuine greatness.

Steve Jobs, entrepreneur, visionary, and legendary founder of the high-tech behemoth Apple, often attributed his uncanny ability to envision what consumers and computer users would want before they knew they wanted it, to his intuition.

Jobs counseled, "Have the courage to follow your heart and intuition. They somehow already know what you truly want to become. Everything else is secondary." He believed that intuition was infinitely more powerful than intellect, and he used those incredible intuitive abilities to tap into his higher self and create one of the largest, most valuable, and most iconic companies in the world.

It is my firm belief that my intuition has led me to this very place I am now, writing this book and living my dream. Each and every decision and experience, whether they were good or bad, happy or sad, easy or difficult, have led me to where I am today and Be Something Wonderful.

All of it was necessary to pave the way to where I am and who I am in this very moment. Now, I intentionally harness my intuition for any major decision I'm going to make.

Tap into your phenomenal superpower. Silence the noise and listen to the voice that always has your best interest in mind. Pay attention to the feelings and synchronicities telling you that you are on the verge of greatness and something marvelous and miraculous is about to happen.

Know that you hold the creative seeds of the Universe in your hands. Dare to dwell in the world of miracles and magic.

Exercise 9 – Intuition

Be Something Wonderful is about seeing the unseen and feeling the unfelt.

In exercise 9, you will access your intuitive center by tapping into universal source energy like you learned in exercises 2 and 4, and then you will measure this connected sensation against your intuitive voice.

1. Close your eyes and take three deep breaths as you focus only on your breathing for a few moments, deeply inhaling through your nose and exhaling through your mouth.

2. Keeping your eyes closed, picture a brilliant white light coming down from above and surrounding your entire body. Feel the warmth and beauty of this light.

3. Now think of a decision you will need to make in the next few days or in the coming weeks.

4. Test a specific outcome of this decision against your inner space. Start with something small and maybe even a decision that you don't consider very significant, and then work your way up as you get more comfortable with your intuitive voice.

For example, "Should I buy those new shoes?" How does it make you feel? If you are feeling anything but a sense of peace, comfort, and confidence in the proposed outcome, you are going against your intuition.

If you are uncertain about how you should feel, look back at a specific decision you have already made that had a really positive outcome. Now revisit the feelings you had when you made this decision–that is exactly how you should feel when you are making decisions with your intuitive center.

Thoughts Are the Formative Force of the Universe

Be Something Wonderful is about uniting with the formative force of loving thoughts.

It's not a coincidence that the final element of The Dare to Be It Code is about thoughts. On the contrary, you now know there are no coincidences or random events. It's all part of your higher self, showing you the way to your awe-inspiring purpose and life's path.

Like everything else in the Universe, thoughts are energy, but carry a much more potent vibration. And when touched by the massive power of emotion—fear or love—they generate the feelings that shape and create your reality.

Buddha, also known as the "Awakened One" and arguably one of history's most prominent spiritual leaders, expressed through his teachings the awesome creative power of thoughts. He enlightened, "We are what we think. All that we are arises with our thoughts. With our thoughts, we make the world." Where you are today, what you are doing right now, and who you are in this very moment was created by your past thoughts.

And what you are believing and thinking right now in this very moment is shaping your next moment, and the next one, and so forth and so on.

Be Something Wonderful has taught me not to fear my thoughts and not to panic or worry when negative thoughts cross my mind. On the contrary, negative thoughts activate fearful feelings and emotions that warn you that you have veered off course—they serve as a powerful contrast to the much more potent emotions of joy, kindness, and love.

They are there to remind you of your innate benevolence. One genuine loving thought can wipe out any negativity that creeps in, because loving thoughts are contagious—one leads to another and then to another, and so on and so forth. It's an amazing divine momentum that feeds your mind, body, and spirit.

Your thoughts, when shaped by your beliefs and infused with love, create the feelings that can bring you endless amounts of joy, happiness, prosperity, and abundance.

If beliefs are the creative seeds of the Universe, then your thoughts are the pure water that makes them stronger and grow, and your emotions are the fertilizer that helps them bloom into beautiful feelings of well-being, joy, compassion, and kindness. Dare to choose thoughts of love, not fear, and connect with the magnificent essence of your higher self.

Exercise 10 - Thoughts

Be Something Wonderful is about waking up to the beautiful, amazing, and magical world that awaits you.

In exercise 10, you are going to practice having *good-feeling* thoughts starting with one joyful thought at a time. Once again, you are going to connect with your higher self, using the methods you learned in exercises 2 and 4, and then build up the power of loving and joyful thoughts from there.

1. Close your eyes and take three deep breaths as you focus only on your breathing for a few moments, deeply inhaling through your nose and exhaling through your mouth.

2. Keeping your eyes closed, picture a brilliant white light coming down from above and surrounding your entire body. Feel the warmth and beauty of this light.

3. Now, get a piece of paper and quickly jot down as many thoughts as possible going through your head.

4. Look at what you have written. How many of those thoughts are positive, affirmative, and helpful to you? How many are negative or unhelpful to you?

5. Instead of trying to avoid or run from negative thoughts, let them come in. But instead of focusing on the negative ones, generate one loving thought and focus on that. And then generate another loving thought and focus on that. One loving thought at a time. You will find it's contagious. When you do this, you shift your focus from the unwanted thoughts to the infinitely more powerful loving thoughts.

Final Thoughts

Be Something Wonderful is seeing the forest for the trees—
reveling in the awesome beauty and divine light that
surrounds you.

Be Something Wonderful is about dwelling in joy and love and in all the inherent goodness abundantly available to you each and every day. Your God-given greatness is lovingly and patiently waiting in the wings for you to show it to the world. It's about making the choice to embrace it, to be more, to be something wonderful.

With *Be Something Wonderful: When Suddenly You Want to Be More,* your real journey has just begun. I am excited and honored to take this journey with you.

If it hasn't happened yet, the Universe will inevitably push and pull you into the direction of your dreams, leading you to make your inevitable jump into your true path and genuine destiny.

Now that your journey has begun, use this amazing, powerful momentum to continue your spiritual transformation and growth. There is no right way or wrong way. Your journey and path is unique to you.

Remember that you are more than enough. Remember that you cannot fail. Remember that you can only learn, transform, and grow.

Be Something Wonderful and the Dare to Be It Code are a reminder of who you truly are—a brilliant and powerful creator of your own unique path and genuine calling.

Relish and enjoy your magical ride into the joyous, unlimited prosperity that the Universe has specifically earmarked for you.

More Be Something Wonderful Wisdom

Be Something Wonderful is about following your inner wanderlust, embarking on the journey of a lifetime.

Be Something Wonderful inspires you to take risks, feeling the freedom of your boundless potential.

Be Something Wonderful empowers you to lead life boldly with strength, purpose, courage, and clarity.

Be Something Wonderful is gentleness, ease, and grace.

Be Something Wonderful is about paving your road to greatness.

Be Something Wonderful is open, innocent, and hopeful.

Be Something Wonderful is about shining a light on that part of you that is so great, so awesome, so pure, so positive—your power, passion, and potential are limitless.

Be Something Wonderful is about trusting what deeply resonates with you.

Be Something Wonderful is about activating your power to heal, transform, and love.

Be Something Wonderful is about busting out from behind the curtain, knowing it's your time. It's your turn. It's your moment.

Be Something Wonderful is about having the courage and confidence to take center stage.

Be Something Wonderful is about taking the spiritual leap, a deep transformation that can feel like heartbreak but is actually your heart expanding, asking for more space to be in.

Be Something Wonderful is that smiley, giddy, giggly feeling of pure joy. Dare to be it™—it just feels good.

Be Something Wonderful is about rising forth into the greatness of which you are made.

Be Something Wonderful is about standing in the certainty of what you can do, in the clarity of who you are, and in the courage of what you can become.

Be Something Wonderful is about filling up with the infinite possibilities of what can be created with love, through love, in love, and by love.

Be Something Wonderful is about waking up to the bliss and promise of a new day.

Be Something Wonderful is when it all makes sense, when it all comes together, when the pieces finally fit.

Be Something Wonderful is the freedom of walking away—embarking on your own journey of goodness and discovery.

Be Something Wonderful is about stepping out of the shadows, touched by the immortal light and invincible energy of what can be.

Be Something Wonderful is about dreaming big–believing that not even the sky is the limit.

Be Something Wonderful is not about what you cling to, but what you let go of.

Be Something Wonderful is about riding that massive wave of enthusiasm and excitement, knowing you are onto something big.

Be Something Wonderful is about stepping up, standing out, and taking your shot.

Be Something Wonderful is about transforming into the invincible leader you are destined to be, taking charge of your own life, doing what you've always dreamed of doing, being whom you've always hoped to be.

Be Something Wonderful is about basking in possibility, knowing the world is your oyster.

Be Something Wonderful is about waking up to the beautiful, amazing, and magical world that awaits you.

Be Something Wonderful is that powerful moment when your life takes off and you stand in awe of what can be.

Be Something Wonderful is that unshakable belief in yourself, feeling the empowering waves of possibility crashing at your feet.

Be Something Wonderful is about making a splash with love, kindness, and compassion.

Be Something Wonderful is about having a voice, speaking up, and being heard.

Be Something Wonderful is the thrill of starting from scratch, writing a new story filled with adventure, love, and hope.

Be Something Wonderful is about leading with strength, courage, and wisdom.

Be Something Wonderful surprises, amazes, and delights.

Be Something Wonderful makes you nimble, graceful, and light on your feet.

Be Something Wonderful is your God-given empowerment to write your own amazing story.

Be Something Wonderful is beautiful, powerful, and graceful.

Be Something Wonderful is mastering the moment, absorbing the glorious rays of your unlimited abundance and endless good fortune.

Be Something Wonderful is about blowing your own horn, showing the world who you are and what you are made of.

Be Something Wonderful is about conquering new heights, rejoicing in the incandescent glow of triumph.

Be Something Wonderful is about embracing the splendor and brilliance of powerful endings, signifying the promise and potential of amazing new beginnings.

Be Something Wonderful raises your spirits and elevates your soul.

Be Something Wonderful is about
embodying the magnificent and magical
power of love, kindness, and compassion.

Be Something Wonderful is the sheer
delight of starting from a blank slate—
leveraging the mighty, creative force of
your thoughts.

Be Something Wonderful is your refuge
from the storm—that peaceful place of
unbridled optimism and immeasurable joy.

Be Something Wonderful is that
unwavering faith that even in your darkest
moments, there exists a pure and almighty
light to sustain and lift us.

Be Something Wonderful lights your way,
calling on your fortitude, resilience, and
grit to forge ahead on your adventurous
road of expansion.

Be Something Wonderful is about graciously lighting the way, being that magnanimous and boundless source of strength, love, and inspiration.

Be Something Wonderful is stoking that fire within, boldly and unabashedly following your heart.

Be Something Wonderful is about dancing between worlds, unleashing your spirit, and celebrating your expansion.

Be Something Wonderful is about knowing that you are enough but aspiring to be more.

Be Something Wonderful is about making your mark—daring to rise to your higher calling.

Be Something Wonderful is that warm
sensation of destiny shining on you,
nudging you in the direction of your
dreams.

Be Something Wonderful is about creating
your own masterpiece—bringing to light the
authentic and amazing you.

Be Something Wonderful reminds you that
you're connected—holding the miraculous
key to it all.

Be Something Wonderful is about tapping
into the fierce and fearless part of you that
dares to be more.

Be Something Wonderful is pure joy, lifting
you to new heights.

Be Something Wonderful is the empowering sensation that it's all in your favor, that life is smiling on you.

Be Something Wonderful returns you to the time and space of carefree innocence and simple pleasures.

Be Something Wonderful is the empowering sensation that it's all in your favor, that life is smiling on you.

Be Something Wonderful is the utter delight of being on cloud nine.

Be Something Wonderful propels you forward, pushing you to grow and expand by leaps and bounds.

Be Something Wonderful is about being in the moment—finding harmony, balance, and peace.

Be Something Wonderful is about chasing rainbows, dreaming the impossible, daring to venture into the new.

Be Something Wonderful is about breathing deeply, feeling massively, loving intensely, and living passionately.

Be Something Wonderful is about remembering that you're connected to the whole shebang.

Be Something Wonderful is about unmasking your omnipotent, benevolent, and loving spirit that dwells within.

Be Something Wonderful is about imagining without limits, wandering with purpose, and living without boundaries.

Be Something Wonderful mesmerizes and enchants with the allure and mystique of new beginnings.

Be Something Wonderful is about following your bliss and shaping your dreams–feeling the magnitude and momentum of your destiny unfolding.

Be Something Wonderful touches your heart and lights up your soul, filling you with the joyous anticipation of all that can be.

Be Something Wonderful is about being that illuminating beacon of hope, insight, and inspiration.

Be Something Wonderful is about expressing the magnanimous whispers of your inner voice.

Be Something Wonderful is about going with the flow, trusting your path, allowing your life to unwrap in the most amazing ways.

Be Something Wonderful is that glorious and triumphant feeling of being on top of the world.

Be Something Wonderful is about uniting with the boundless brilliance, supreme power, and divine guidance of your higher self.

Be Something Wonderful is that angelic reflection of your inherent greatness and blessed life still to come.

Be Something Wonderful is about returning to your timeless goodness within and writing a fresh, new script of boundless potential.

Be Something Wonderful is about standing firmly in your belief that the Universe has an amazing plan for you.

Be Something Wonderful is that powerful yet subtle step moments before your ideas take flight and your destiny is unveiled.

Be Something Wonderful is about getting back into the swing of life, indulging in the moment, taking delight in the little things.

Sources

*Be Something Wonderful is gaining that all-powerful,
celestial perspective that you got this.*

- Braden, Gregg. *The Divine Matrix: Bridging Time, Space, Miracles, and Beliefs.* 2007. Hay House, Inc.

- Chopra, Deepak. *The Seven Spiritual Laws of Success.* 1994. Amber-Allen Publishing and New World Library.

- Danes, Chuck. Abundance-and-Happiness.com. 2005-2012.

- Dooley, Mike. *Infinite Possibilities: The Art of Living Your Dreams.* 2009. Atria Books, A Division of Simon & Schuster, Inc. and Beyond Words.

- Dotts, Richard. *Inner Confirmation for Outer Manifestations.* 2015. 1st Kindle Edition.

- Dotts, Richard. *The Magic Feeling Which Creates Instant Manifestations.* 2015. 2nd Kindle Edition.

- Dyer, Wayne. *The Power of Intention: Learning to Co-Create Your World Your Way.* 2004. Hay House, Inc.

- Dyer, Wayne. *Wishes Fulfilled: Mastering the Art of Manifesting.* 2012. Hay House, Inc.

- Esther and Jerry Hicks (The Teachings of Abraham). *Ask and It Is Given: Learning to Manifest Your Desires.* 2004. Hay House, Inc.

- Esther and Jerry Hicks (The Teachings of Abraham). *The Law of Attraction: The Basic Teachings of Abraham.* 2006 Hay House, Inc.

- Gawain, Shakti. *Developing Intuition.* 2000. Nataraja Publishing, A Division of New World Library.

- Kuhn, Greg. *How Quantum Physicists Build New Beliefs.* 2013. Kindle Direct Publishing Edition

- McTaggart, Lynne. *The Field: The Quest for the Secret Force of the Universe.* 2008. HarperCollins eBooks.

- Rankin, Lissa. "8 Signs You've Lost Touch with Your Intuition." 2016. Mindbodygreen. com.

- Robbins, Anthony. *Awaken the Giant Within: How to Take Immediate Control of Your Mental, Emotional, Physical, and Financial Destiny.* 1991. Free Press, A Division of Simon & Schuster, Inc.

- St. Maarten, Anthon. *Divine Living: The Essential Guide to Your True Destiny.* 2012. Indigo House, South Africa.

- Walia, Arun. *The Illusions of Matter: Our Physical Material World Isn't Really Physical at All.* 2013.

About the Author

Once you unveil that, once you discover, once you shine a light on that part of you that is so great, so awesome, so pure, so positive—your passion, power, and potential are limitless.

Tom Kearin, Founder &
CEO of Be Something Wonderful

Tom Kearin, born in 1963, grew up in Chelmsford, Massachusetts, just thirty miles north of Boston in the Merrimack Valley.

Raised by a widowed alcoholic mother after his father died when he was just six years old, Tom struggled to find his place among a family of seven kids. Growing up on welfare and food stamps in an environment of chaos and dysfunction, Tom intuitively there must be something more.

As many of his siblings dropped out of high school and battled with drug and alcohol abuse, and while his mother taunted him to quick college, get a job, and "be like the others," Tom battled his way through university, graduating in 1986 and entering the business world as an assistant auditor at KPMG Peat Marwick in Boston.

As Kearin looks back now, none of it quite felt right. From college to his career in business, he always had the sense that he was different, and destined to do more and to be more.

As the years went by, the "sensitive one" began discovering and feeling an inevitable pull toward spirituality and the mystery and magic of the Universe.

Finally, in January 2016, after a lifetime in business and executive leadership positions with one foot in the physical world and one foot in the spiritual world, the calling became loud enough and strong enough for Tom to take the spiritual leap and launch Be Something Wonderful.

Tom is a passionate, high-energy international entrepreneur, consultant, coach, advisor, mentor, teacher, and trainer. His business leadership spans a variety of industries, including technology, computer manufacturing, accounting and audit, business consulting, and international study abroad and educational travel. Tom has held various corporate roles as an auditor, financial controller, treasurer, chief financial officer, chief operating officer, president, chief executive officer, board member, and shareholder.

Tom has a Bachelor of Science in Business Administration and an MBA in Finance. He started his career as an auditor in KPMG Peat Marwick in Boston with Certified Public Accountant certificates in the states of Massachusetts, California, and Nevada. Tom is fluent in Spanish and spent the last twelve years dividing his time between the United States and Latin America as a partner and the chief operating officer in an international study abroad and educational travel company.

Inspired and overwhelmed with his true calling, he left Latin America in August 2017, returning to the United States to dedicate all of his energy and time to Be Something Wonderful. Tom now resides in Carlsbad, California.

Be Something Wonderful

If you had any idea how bright your tomorrows will be, you would be celebrating each ending, marveling at every sunset, and standing in awe of the epic blessings yet to come.

Be Something Wonderful LLC, a Nevada limited liability company founded in January 2016, offers a fresh, new approach to life coaching and consulting that blends business and spirituality, creating a platform for transformative training that lifts, inspires, and motivates you to be the best version of yourself in business as well as in life.

Be Something Wonderful's umbrella of programs and services include life and corporate coaching, personal and spiritual wellness, executive leadership training and consulting, educational seminars and services, and more.

For more information visit:

- TomKearin.com
- Twitter & Instagram: @tomkearin
- Facebook: @tomkearinllc

Printed in Great Britain
by Amazon

53078976R00068